THE FOOL'S MIRROR

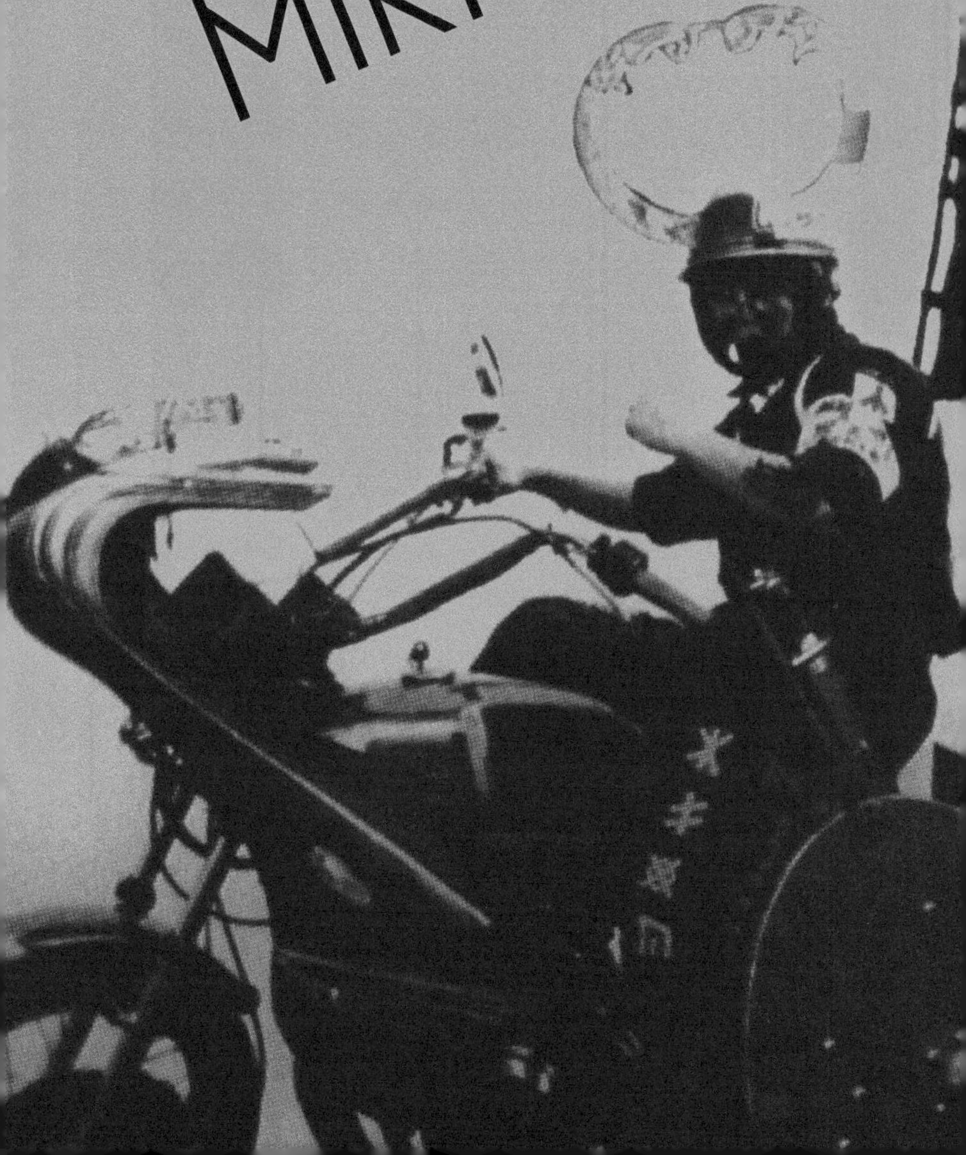

Contact

Brutenorse@gmail.com

Brutenorse.com

Linktr.ee/brutenorse

Instagram & Twitter

@brutenorse

Issue 1

● Heyannir 2022

Cover illustration by Didrik Magnus-Andresen

Back cover image by Eirik Irgens Johnsen,

ISBN: 979-8-9863430-0-6

My humblest thanks to

Jake, Michael, KB, the Scandifuturist Powerwalking Club, and all of the contributors

IN THIS ISSUE

Chronicles

Art & Poetry

Lifestyle

IT IS 100 SECONDS
TO MIDNIGHT
Norway faces butter shortage
Troll

Editorial

A Mirror for Fools

n the 1270's, Hákon Hákonarsson, king of he Norwegian realm, commissioned a tome of courtly miscellanea for the education of his son Magnus. Written as a socratic dialogue between father and son, it served as a primer on a wide arrangement of subjects that a young noble might need on his path to becoming ruler: courtly etiquette, best practices for doing business, diplomacy, science, military tactics, and the economic resources of the realm's extremities. To liven things up, it also contained curiosities from across the North Atlantic, including a variety of natural and supernatural wonders. And so it was dubbed Kónungs Skuggsjá: The King's Mirror.

The King's Mirror finds itself in an established European tradition of didactic literature. Of mirrors of this and that. There, the anonymous scribe brings the reader up to speed with the ideas of his time. But also expressing desire to have his work presented more widely: to not ust face the court, but benefit the commoner as well, for the perpetuation of good habits, wisdom and know-how. The primordial idea with my other project, Brute Norse, was to break away from the cage of institutional academia and contribute to the realization and acculturation of New Museology. Towards new, perhaps foolhardy, but hopefully robust paradigms. To produce scholarly outreaches among the barbarians, and for myself to become a nomadic war machine. A heretic who dwells out in the steppes and ungovernable margins amongst the proverbial Scythians and Goths.

It is completelty foolish, of course, but people underestimate fools. Fools are the mirror images of kings. Odin, the Norse aristocratic god of war, wisdom, intoxication and sorcery, often appears in a fool's aspect. He is Apollo and Dionysus as one and same. A god of institutions who subverts.

In an age where the flow of information will inevitably erode the fortresses and ivory towers of traditional academia, and where initiation is attainable to every barbarian, this self-vulgarization is a natural and needed step forward in the world of antiquarian scholarship. To me this is not about pushing that which is already falling, for in many ways I am sympathetic to the monastic isolationism of academic tradition. But the center will not hold, and those scholars who don't already find themselves out in the wasteland in their dune buggies competing with autodidacts, will do it soon enough. Better to do as the good old Ash Farter of the Norwegian fairy tales, the foolish young son who levels the playing field and outcompetes his less vulgar, well-adjusted brothers by allying himself with trolls, hags, and other agents of chaos. Who, by facing up to the circumstances, earns the princess and half the kingdom.

So what's the plot? Where do I want to go with this «Scandifuturism» business? Will they find us one day in a compound, voluntarily expired, all wearing identical birch bark clogs in some folkloric likeness of Heaven's Gate? How much kool-aid does one have to drink to be a Scandifuturist anyway? Do we really need another product spewing from the conveyor belt of the Scandinavian Concept Industrial Complex? Scandifuturism willed itself into existence as a way for me to express my general approach to things, since none of the currents out there seemed to suit my needs and motivations. Without a clear vision of who my audience might be, I began to think of this unseen blob as The Invisible Choir. And as I preached, people emerged who shared many of my dissatisfacations.

Scandifuturism by its very definition uses speculative reality and surrealism as an

aesthetic-philosophical device. This in return was borrowed from the morbidly humorous memetic techniques employed by Skaldic poets in the pre-Christian Era. A grotesque aesthetic ideal where opposites attract and conjoin in creative impulse. The mutant as aesthetic ideal. Through this we desire to tear down the modern delusion that past and present are like oil and water, never touching. In fact, I would argue that such historicist lies are what paved way for some of the grossest abuses of cultural heritage of the past few centuries.

The past is being produced all the time, and is in fact indistinguishable from the present. The letters spilling from my keyboard right now are tainted by the passing of time faster than I can type. The absurdity of the idea of the present, that it is strictly in the present that we live, and that this presentness by some timely prison cordons us off in temporal space, is self-evidently false. Epistemically idiotic. There is not a moment where the living human does not experience the past. That is where we live, and from whence everything comes and makes its way into the world. Though our sensory perception fools us into thinking we experience anything in real time, everything we perceive has already happened by the time we realize it has. What we mean by the present is more usually our relative chronological context. A temporal space that is more or less contemporary to our lived experience, true, but the fact remains that all our lived experiences are derivative. As we know full and well that living in the present is impossible, we allow for some pragmatic leeway. Yesterday, last decade, tomorrow, next year, are all relatively current. The narrative present of the modern myth, anyway. But this relative chronology is inevitably muddled up with the past, and is doomed to pollute our perception of it, as any chapter of research history or any snapshot of popular culture will inevitably demonstrate.

I am not so concerned with telling people what exactly Scandifuturism is supposed to be, though I will make multiple attempts at exemplifying it in this issue. As this is the first issue of hopefully many, I may come at risk of forcing my points across. Then again, in the spirit of example, most of the contents in this zine were penned by yours truly, so please bear with him. My general idea is that this magazine will serve to be an outlet. One of many potential ones – many of which should probably be completely disconnected from myself – that will serve as a venue to encourage a Scandifuturistic point of view. For Scandifuturism is also its own animal. Not even I really understand, or seek to understand, or fully explain what it is. To some people, Scandifuturism is practiced by exercising folk culture. They wear woolen sweaters and pick berries mindfully and whatnot.

Others consider it strictly as a way of seeing, or some sort of machine to produce novelty and superstitions. Heritage, I suppose, is an inescapable aspect. To reject modern materialism, and to open the mind and heart to experiences beyond the confines of contemporary sentiments and priorities, and to see oneself in a wider continuum. To combat cultural amnesia and promote cultural heritage. But in doing this, also avoiding the pitfalls that many make who reject the reality of the modern condition. Scandifuturists do not try to live in the past, because they realize they are already doing it. Foolish? Yes. This is why I decided to make this magazine.

A mirror by fools, for fools.

LAT · OSS · IKKJE
FORFEDRANE · GLØYMA
UNDER · ALT · SOM
ME · VENDA · OG · SNU

Chronicles

Eirik Storesund

THE LIFTERS OF THE STONES

A report on stones and the folk who lift them.

In Norway, only a pathetic 3% of the landmass is arable. Whoever has had the mixed pleasure of living and/or dying off the land will agree that rocks are one thing this land will not be running out of any time soon. Shifting rocks was synonymous with farming to such a degree that people who weren't fortunate enough to possess a plot of land where some distant ancestor had already shifted the worst of it, very often resorted to calling their land Ruð as a testament to the prerequisite work. From Old Norse ryðja meaning «to clear up, tidy». Being around rocks all the time, constantly wrestling with the natural landscape, may leave an imprint on any person. Scale that up to entire societies, you just develop a culture of stone bothering. I know I have felt absurd joy from shifting big rocks out of my potato patch and defiantly rolling them off the hillside as punishment for their natural sins. After bringing this up, my friend argued that natural stones have a very trollish feeling. They actively resist being lifted, throwing you off balance and slipping out of your hands at every opportunity. I agree, the tension is mutual. That just as I have bothered the stones, certainly there are stones that are perched patiently, waiting thousands of years for someone like me to come by. Bothered or unbothered, but none the less awaiting the right time to slip out of place and crush many a bone in my body. Perhaps even take my life, but at the very least mangle me for good. In an odd mirror fashion, trolls, the eternal shadow of the Scandinavian soul, were sometimes thought to pelt and tip stones. To rain them down upon people in wanton thirst for suffering, as if commenting in their own way on the reciprocal nature of human-trollish comorbidity.

-Art by Olof Hanvark / @olofhanvark

In this strange relationship, there is also an aspect of appreciation. If the mountain crashes down on top of me while I sleep, I would not only have to accept but respect it. Even though on an individual basis, assuming agency, this would make for a rather asymmetrical retaliation for the few stones of note that I have managed to smash in my lifetime, or made brittle in the heat of bonfires and sauna stoves. Which by the way are much fewer than I would have liked.

There is a certain chivalry, a sense of honor. I love the sight of a good rock. I respect its stoic, trollish disposition. Indifferent. Hot or cold only depending on the season. Slap your hand on it like a well fed hog. Perhaps it is really out of a sort of appreciation that I like to pick them up sometimes, just to show them who is boss. To lean into my humanity, my cognitively hardwired anthropocentrism which compels me to at least pretend I am not just an insignificant and arbitrary fleshbot of divine design, spitefully slung into this sandbox by the gods.

I am not much of a strongman either, it has to be said. Løfte stein. Løftestein. Løfte løftestein. Common vernacular variant; lyftestein. Odd to put this in plain English. Lifting stones. Lifting stones. Lifting lifting stones. Something is lacking.

Anyway. It is rare for a monument to be as interactive, and to continue encouraging interaction on such an intuitive level. Across Norway, there are many renowned stones which possess this odd charisma. That they are of an appropriate size and shape, that people look at them and reckon that they make for a suitable measure of a single man's strength (real or ideal), that they are integrated into local culture and given apt names such as: Lyftesteinen. «The Lifting Stone». That, or some variant, appears to be the most common, but other terms, and faint memories of other terms exist. In Shetland Norn, for example, there was a term bragasten, indicating the elusive existence of an unattested Old Norse *bragðasteinn (literally «stone of feats»). Another indirect case speaking for the esteem of rock bothering in Norse culture may be seen in the cautionary proverb taka stein um megin – «to take a stone beyond your strength» (Which appears in Færeyinga saga).

The earliest mention of one such actual stone in Scandinavia, at least that I can recall from the top of my head, is certainly the stone referenced in the legendary saga of king Hálfr Hjorleifsson of Hordaland. A man so strong that none were his equal, even though he was actually a twelve year old child, if the saga is to be believed. It was at this tender age that Hálfr decided to prepare for a viking raid that was to last 18 years. He set up a wide range of unrealistic expectations that each of his champions had to adhere to. Among the less unreasonable was the first: that they had to be able to lift a certain stone at his court that could ordinarily only be lifted by twelve regular

Steinlyftet on Lyftehøgd'n in Nord-Aurdal. Photo: Knut Hermundstad / Valdres Folkemuseum

Joes. Among his men there were two brothers, both called Steinn, which incidentally means «Stone». Apparently his immediate milieu was quite enthused by geology.

A number of renowned lifting-stones are known to have existed in later centuries, and still do, though intergenerational amnesia may have retired unspoken numbers to indefinite obscurity. A semantic note: what qualifies as a lyftestein on its most basic, material level as «stone of certain size» is not clearly defined. In Ivar Aasen's Ordbog over det norske Folkesprog (Dictionary of the Norwegian vernacular), whereby urbanists and trustees of the Danish tongue might disseminate the savage babble of their rural Norwegian brethren, a lyftestein is defined simply as «a heavy stone which serves as a test of strength, in that several man compete in lifting it.» Internal newsletters for Norwegian builders in the 20th century reveal attempts at codifying lyftestein as a technical term for stones of a certain distinction that qualifies builders to receive extra compensation for moving them. A natural concern in their vocation. In some cases, it is apparent that writers of topographical and archaeological literature will refer to any stone over a certain size as lyftestein if the following criteria are met: that it has obviously been moved by human hands, and that most people would find it challenging.

In other words it is a matter of knowing it when you see it. Such is the case with all the Bronze and Iron Age cairns that dot the country, as well as many hillforts, which consist of stones of varying size. Many certainly large enough to have proven a challenge for one single man to lift on their own, let alone across distances and uphill into awkward but obvious positions in the landscape, and then multiplied several times over. The term doesn't necessarily imply stones of a certain shape, though rounded stones and stones with a striking, natural morphology that allows one to grip them a certain way, or actually makes them harder to grip, have certainly encouraged individual stones to emerge before mortal eyes as stones to be lifted for sport.

In an Early Iron Age barrow cemetery at Hunn in Østfold, a cup mark stone is supposed to have had a home on top of one of the burial mounds, where it was apparently used in recent historical memory as a lyftestein. One legend recounts a case of Odinic inversion, in which Olaf the holy traveled around the country in the guise of a beggar, testing commoners as he went. One day he met a miserly lady roasting flatbreads who refused to give him any. So he turned the dough into a rock, which people felt compelled to lift ever since. Commonly these stones become the pride of a specific area. Other cases are less tied to place: in one instance, a lyftestein occasionally served part-time as ballast for a boat, but that seems to be an exception.

Sterke-Nils-steinen (The Strong Nils Stone) is a stone you can still visit in Seljord, Telemark, and which was lifted by the eponymous Nils Olsen Langedal some time in the mid 18th century. It is said that six men originally tried to move the stone in order to put it in the wall of a local fortress, but Nils asked them to step aside and lifted it easily, though he sank to his ankles in the ground. The stone weighs 570 kilos. Additionally there are two separate stones, in Seljord and Kviteseid respectively tied to is name, both called Klypelyftsteinen (The Pinch Grip Stone). The selling point of either being that they demonstrate grip strength. One being 75 kilos, the other 120. The heavier is now mounted to a base which bears a plaque to Strong Nils, «born in Kviteseid in 1721, beaten to death in Seljord in the year 1800». Haddemohadden in Haddemo, also in Telemark, is about 350 kilos and was lifted by Olav «Storegut» Olavsson Edland, who lived between 1764 and 1791. Another stone is supposed to have been lifted in Kvistad in Møre og Romsdal by the then 18 year old Jakob E. Kvistad (1871-1943). The stone weighs 398.5 kilos.

Lyftesteinar (plural) also served other purposes and unexpected purposes. Among the many ways one could divine a future spouse in vernacular magic, was by wading backwards in a creek that runs north. Reach backwards for a stone: if you don't have the strength to lift it, you will not get the one you desire, or you might not even get hitched at all. If the stone is uneven, you will marry someone ugly. If it is smooth, your spouse will be beautiful.

Read more

about lifting stones at
https://liftingstones.org

Need a little help?

«Whereby, in a natural way, one may take the strength of a horse and transplant it into a human being»

According to the Cyprianus manuscript NB Ms. 8° 10, c. 1790

Take the seed of nature from a stallion, which one may gather from the mares as they release it. Mix it with good soil and plant therein a plant called «Camelseangerum». Let it grow, and give it to a human to eat, hang it around their neck, and have them share chambers with the horse: then the horse becomes weak while the man becomes strong. But the root one shall replant immediately after the new moon, and 2 or 3 days before the new moon that is to follow, one is to dig it back up. In the same way one may take the power from other animals and share it with the person as aforementioned. And this transplant is most certain, and well concealed in secrecy.

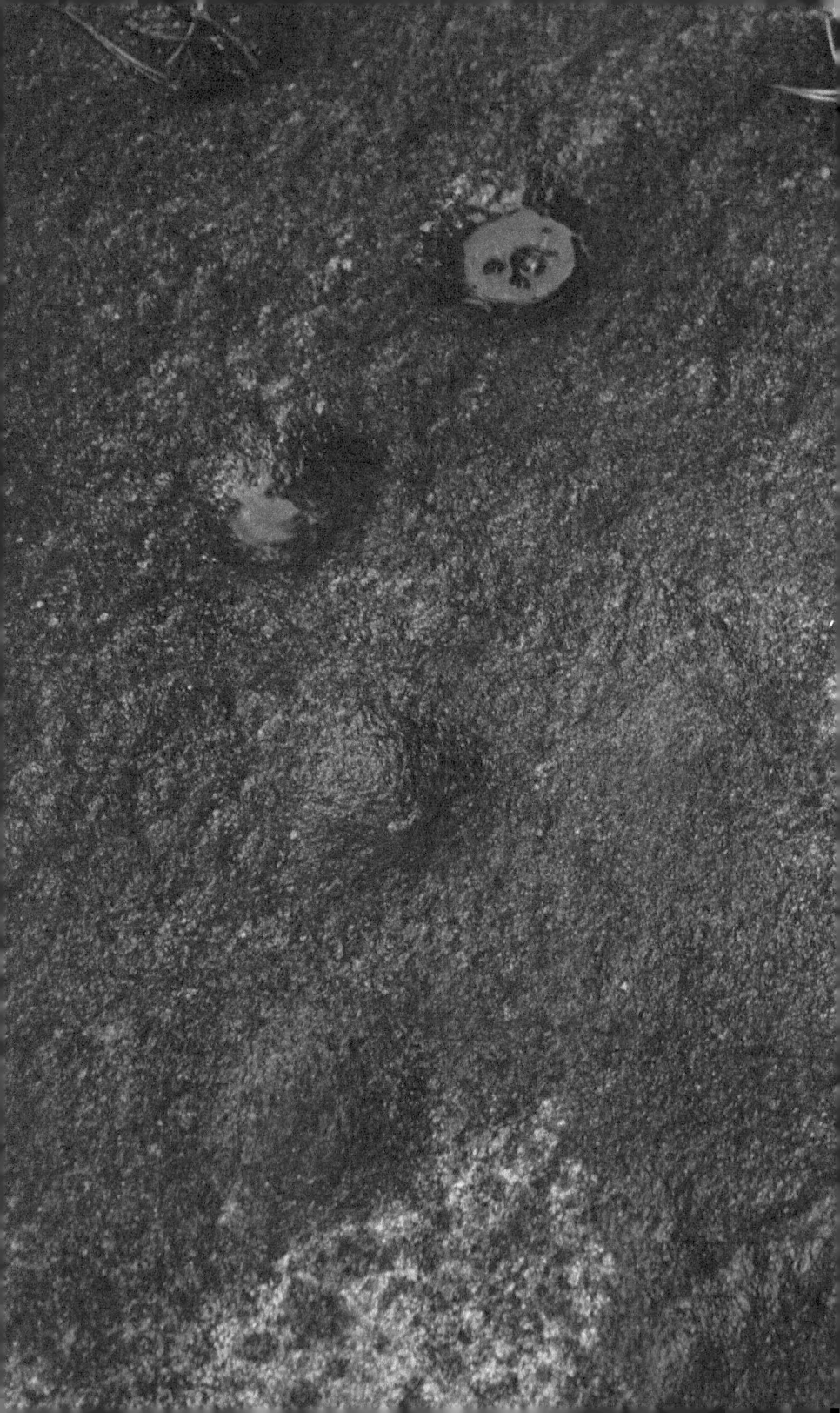

THE FINAL GREASING OF THE ELF-QUERNS

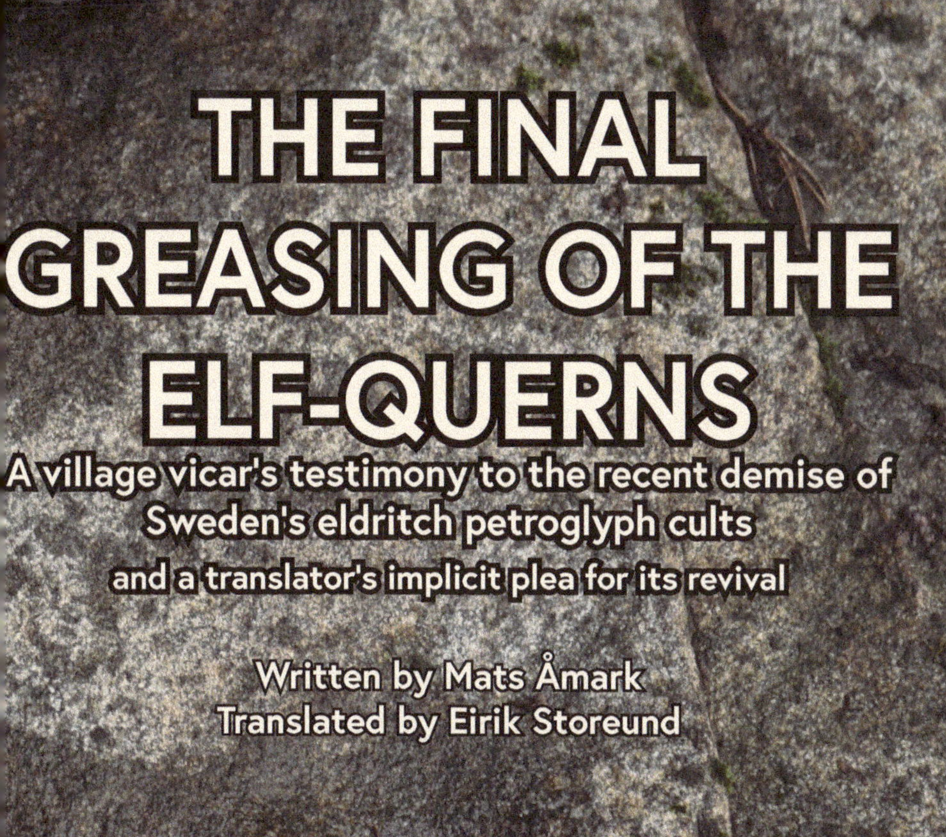

A village vicar's testimony to the recent demise of Sweden's eldritch petroglyph cults

and a translator's implicit plea for its revival

Written by Mats Åmark
Translated by Eirik Storeund

I cannot prove that the elf-querns I saw greased in the summer of 1923 truly were the last ones in this country that were treated in the ancestral way. It is very possible of course, and even likely, that some of those priestesses – if we can call them that – who practiced these clandestine rites, continued to grease and sacrifice. But when I had the opportunity to investigate some of these old cult sites a couple of decades later, moss and lichen had already coated the elf-querns, once glistening with fat.

The ancient custom was still alive in southern Uppland as late as 1923, specifically in certain parishes in Trögd Hundred, south of Enköping. And I have reason to suspect, that this even then ancient peasant district was the last place in our country where you really could see elf-querns that were still in use. Properly greased with fat, and votive deposits just as it had been for centuries. This presumption of mine is based on the testimony of one particular scholar who has devoted in-depth research to the aforementioned cult practice. Oskar Lidén mentions in his Hällgröpningsstudier (1938) that he has found lots of elf-querns, especially in Småland and Västergötland, but none which were in use. During a research trip to Uppland, with visits to the areas north of Enköping, he had also, in spite of his hopes, failed to find any elf-querns that were still in use. In the areas south of Enköping he supposedly had better luck in the research of what he calls «hällgröpningar», a name that however is alien to Uppland. Within the area I am most familiar with, quite thoroughly researched by the national antiquarian, I have never heard these ancient monuments in question be referred to by another name besides elf-quern.

The name presumably comes from the fact that the cultic act, if we can call it that, for the most part went such that the one sacrificing in the elf-querns, or cup marks[1], swirled a piece of pork rind or a fat-drenched cloth in a movement that immediately recalls how the women in olden days turned the millstone on the old rotary querns. Still in the years of crisis during the first world war I experienced that such ancient rotary stone querns were used to grind grain, when for whatever reason people didn't wish to take the grain to the mill. It was the common understanding that the elf-querns were greased up and served as receptacles for offerings in honor of the elves. The term elf-quern appears to have referred both to the stone or slab in its entirety, with their various little craters, as well as the individual elf-bowls which were greased. One sought in this way to appease the elves, these secretive little

[1] Corresponds to the more common Scandinavian term, skålgrop: «bowl pit».

creatures, whose vengeance one had been «struck by».

I have not made these reflections about the cultic performance itself based on my own thoughts. Few, if any, now living person would have witnessed the «anointing» of elf-querns. This always occurred in great secrecy, and my knowledge about it is received second-hand. I actually had, as I will later reveal, the fortune to encounter and question a former «priestess». That she unlike her fellow sisters was so keen to share, relied entirely on the fact that she had abandoned her work, and subsequently thought that she could laugh about it. Therefore I will leave be the various theories and ponderings on the origins of, and the historical religious significance of these magical acts, to instead recollect what I have personally heard and seen of the elf-querns of Uppland.

Just a few words about the cult sites themselves. Of elf-querns or cup marks, if you so prefer to call them, there are two kinds to be distinguished. At least in Uppland. In part they occur on outcrops protruding from the earth, of which the southern parts are particularly rich, often along striations from the Ice Age. On such slabs it's possible to find a large amount of bowls, either in groups or spread between images of ships or other Bronze Age carvings, which are also typical of these districts. But there are also slabs that contain elf-querns only, so they don't always appear in tandem with other petroglyphs. But as a rule it could be said that if you would like to find images of ships and other Bronze Age petroglyphs, then you should look for these where there are elf-querns, then as bowl-shaped depressions in bedrock. The other sort of elf-querns occur on loose stones or boulders. In this case it appears that only cup marks occur, and no figures. During the years where I have had the chance to observe elf-querns it appears that both types were used. More or less depending on whichever sort was most accessible to those sacrificing, as far as I can discern.

It is obvious that the use of elf-querns in the 1910's and 1920's was in decline. Only here and there could you find an elf-quern still in use. If you asked someone, middle-aged or older, about such things it was usually said that «that was before, that was» when this or that old woman went and greased. And utmost of the elf-querns had for longer or shorter time stood unused, by which moss and lichen had come to cover both stones, and slabs, and elf-bowls.

It was at a birthday party down in the district of Trögden around 1912 where we came to chat about the customs and practices of olden days. As for myself I had recently moved to those tracts as a newly appointed assistant vicar in Kunghusby parish by Veckholm pastorate. One of my schoolmates from the secondary school in Enköping, now a farmer in Hacksta parish, happened to mention that he had an elf-quern on his property. We decided that I should pay him a visit so that we could both inspect this ancient site. I had likely heard spoken of elf-querns before, but I had no clear image of what it was. Now I was about to witness one still in use.

My friend B. received me with care. After coffee we went to the pasture where he wanted to show me his elf-quern, and indeed the stone lay there in a wooded slope which ended down by a field. On the surface one could see a a great many round, somewhat shallow, bowl-shaped depressions, which bore witness to the fact that they had, perhaps even newly, been smeared with fat.

– I had heard it said that the old lady Johansson used go here on Thursday nights, said B., and so I went there myself one evening at dusk. The stone lay as it does now, and all the bowls were empty. I went and sat a bit further away, hidden by some bushes while I waited for the old lady to arrive. But when nobody appeared and it began to get late, I decided to go home. But first I went ahead to the stone, and can you imagine! It had been greased with suet, and in the hollows there were pennies. Since then I have been at watch there on several Thursday nights to get wind of the old lady, but it proved impossible. The stone was greased every time, but no crone appeared. She must have crawled her way through the grass between the juniper trees!

My fascination for these peculiar, ancient monuments was now awakened. As the delegate of the national antiquarian for Trögd Hundred I considered myself to have a certain responsibility to further investigate their occurrence in the district. So eventually I would also succeed in getting to see more of these old cult sites in use. In the autumn of 1913 I was made aware that a large elf-quern was supposed to exist in the hamlet of Kynge in Veckholm parish. It lay in a pasture and was found to be a stone slab, longer than a meter, which barely rose above the surrounding grassy plain. Along the center part of the stone could be seen a row of round hollows, small and large. Around the holes there were whole dabs of pork suet, and in their bowls there were needles and small copper coins, but I never came to investigate who greased them.

In the middle of Trögd there are the two parishes of Lillkyrka and Boglösa. It was during the years (1917-1924) when I acted as vicar in this pastorate that I made the best finds of these ancient monuments which are of interest to us. In the village of Hässlinge in Lillkyrka there lived an old and talkative man, who was a pastry chef in his youth, but had returned to his family farm. With slight irony, though with no small amount of ancestral carefulness, he willingly imparted things from older times.

– There was an old lady named Wall. She was a almswoman who lived here in Hässlinge. Whenever she got ill, she would go to the elf-quern and put down a penny. She used to leave one of those coppers. But if she washed herself

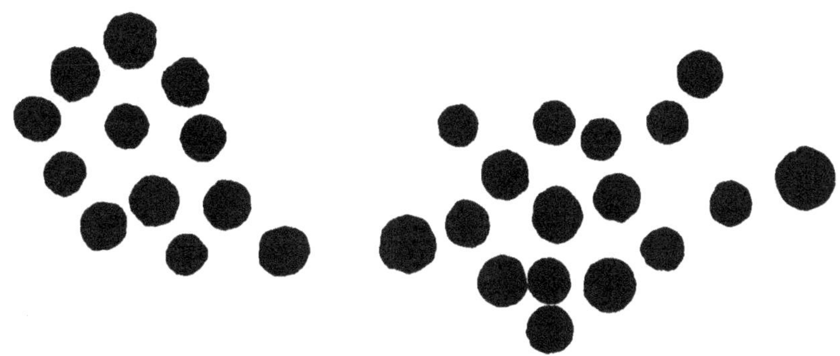

n the water in the hole, or if she had it there sic], I don't know.

The elf-quern in question was situated by a mall farm with the beautiful name Kallkälla. Here we can discern a somewhat different custom than how it was with the previous elf-querns. In those cases, empty cup marks were greased up, whereupon offerings were left. But here my informant claimed that the one who sacrificed had used the rainwater which collects in the hole.

Numerous sacrificial stones of this kind, derivative so to speak of the elf-querns proper, existed in the district. Usually called «wart-stones» or «wart-springs». One such stone in Hässlinge, even mentioned by the pastry chef, was a lesser boulder by the road. On its top surface was a cavity about ten centimeters in diameter. The rainwater which collected in the hole was considered good against warts. The use of these wart-stones was clearly not limited to any special sacrificing old lady, that is: a priestess. The pastry chef told of the wart-stone in his hometown: «As soon as someone hurt themselves, they have gone to the stone and washed themselves in the water that was in the opening. Then afterwards they lay a quarter shilling in it. If they didn't find any water, they'd bring it.»

Such wart-stones or wart-springs existed in several places in Trögden, such as one on the farm of Hornö in Vallby parish. An older woman told about it:

– People who were bothered by warts would on a moonlit Thursday night circumambulate the stone with as many peas in their hand as they had warts. The peas were sowed out while the following was uttered:

I sow and I sow
I sow away my warts

When the peas sprouted, the warts would go away. However, I never got to see this wart-stone on Hornö, and its ceremonies were by the 1920's already lost to the past. Hence I did not find out if any submersion of the fingers in rainwater occurred at this stone. This had however happened in the wart-spring situated in a large slab of bedrock on the fields of my own rectory in the village of Östersta in Kunghusby parish. It consisted of a rather narrow, couple of centimeters long, and rather deep hole in a larger, naked piece of rock. The whole was always full of water, and a small flat stone lay on top of the hole. As far as I know, this «wart-spring» was not used in the years (1912-1917) we lived in Östersta, and I never heard about how it went when it was previously used. It lived on only in name.

Our closest neighboring parish, Boglösa, which was simultaneously my annex parish, was a genuine peasant parish with about 800 inhabitants across several hamlets. There were elf-querns in just about every hamlet there. In Svallby, neighboring Lillkyrka, a middle-aged freeholder told what he could recall about the village elf-quern, which no longer existed, but had nevertheless been used a bit into this century.

– There was a big stone on our farm where the pig pen is now. The stone was full of elf-querns all over. The old women went there and greased. They even came from Hävlinge in Lillkörka. The old lady Hoffsten used to go early in the mornings to grease. Father got angry and blew the stone up. It made a grea foundation for the new pig pen.

During a visit to the nearby hamlet of Blacksta I found that one of the cornerstones on a newl built lodge had a whole heap of elf-quern hollows. Here as well some non-believers hac apparently found the hamlet's old elf-quern fi for a more modern purpose.

Not far from both of the aforementioned hamlets there is one called Kumla. In a field a few hundred meters away from the village, very close to the road, I found an outcrop that hac been used as an elf-quern. The cup marks were quite shallow and not entirely circular. Lichen had already begun to cover the old offering stone, whose elf-querns had apparently been out of use for several years. Villagers recalled however, how the old lady Tapper from the neighboring village of Gådi used to go there and grease. She had names for the holes: One she called Stora grytan [The big pot], another Lilla grytan [The small pot]. The old lady had always greased three holes in a session three times in each hole. She would go when Thursday evening arrived, and always greased against the direction of the sun. The first and last evening she lay a needle or a small copper

coin in the holes she had greased. For each swirl the old lady said:

I grease stone
To heal flesh and bone.

This woman could tell me that when she was younger, she got to go with the old lady Tapper when she greased. It was also here in the village of Kumla that I encountered the woman, who was willing to impart how she herself had greased elf-querns.

– See, I greased, the widow Tilda told, for the husband's swollen legs. First the legs were anointed by the stove. Nine Thursday nights in a row should it be, and every time you said:

I grease bone and not stone

Then you went out at dusk. You weren't allowed to say anything if you encountered anyone. And three hollows on the elf-quern should be greased with an unsalted piece of pork rind, three times in each hollow, and then you said:

I grease stone
to heal flesh and bone.

When mother Tilda told of this her husband had already been dead for several years. What effect the greasing had, I did not find out.

We had now come a bit into the 1920's, and the elders in the hamlets who could recall old times began to die off. I thought that the widow in Kumla was the last practitioners of the old cult one in those parishes. Therefore it was a surprise when I heard about an elf-quern that was apparently still in use in Boglösa, one of our closest neighboring villages. It was barely two and a half kilometers from our rectory in Lillkyrka to Utmyrby, where supposedly there was a greased elf-quern. But I suspected that

it wouldn't be easy to find. People didn't gladly speak with the priest about such matters. So I asked some children who were playing on the road if they knew about any elf-quern.

– «Well yes, auntie greases for the eyes», the kids replied. I understood right away who the aunt was: An old pious widow that I had visited several times, and who went to church frequently. She did really have, I recalled, eyes that were red around the edges, and the good woman had therefore, just to be on the safe side, kept to the old customs. It wasn't easy to know if one had «been struck» with something. Perhaps she had forgetfully poured some hot water on the ground, and thus angered the small beings, who were considered easily upset and vindictive. With the children as my guide I soon stood beside the distinguished old elf-quern of the hamlet. It lay in a forest hillside a bit on the outskirts. On a long and sloping piece of mountain, worn and polished by the glaciers of the Ice Age with deep striations, appeared a long row. Hollow by hollow. And in a couple of them which appeared to be freshly greased, there were both needles and small change! «Auntie» herself, the old priestess who «greased for the eyes», I did not want to bother with any questions. Therefore I never found out how she went about when she sacrificed in elf-quern, or which words she then presumably used.

This memoir must be concluded with a strange experience by an elf-quern in Trögd from a later visit there, many years later. In the end of the 40's I visited one summer my old congregations to say hello to old friends. At the same time I also wanted very much to survey some of the ancient sites here described, and see if any of them were still in use. It turned out as I suspected, however. The round, once so clean and with fat glistening elf-querns were now again overgrown by moss and lichen. It was obvious that they had been out of use for a long time.

I had just photographed the previously mentioned stone in Kynge, when I slipped on the white moss on the adjacent rock. With the camera in my hand I fell and hurt myself so bad, that only with the greatest difficulty could I carry myself out of there. The physician who later looked at me considered it almost a wonder that I didn't break my leg.

Perhaps it was the revenge of the elves?

This article was originally published as *När de sista älvkvarnarna smordes* in Rig 39, no. 3 (1956): 5

Tjernagel, meaning «Sword Nail», was a Bronze Age cairn, already 2000 years old when the skald Þórarinn loftunga mentioned it in 1028. The oldest clearly attested name for any burial mound. It was dynamited in 1983 to make room for radio masts that would stand for only 25 years before they were deemed obsolete.

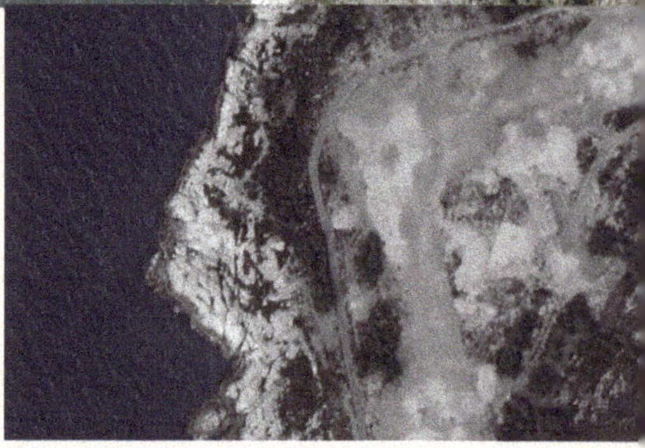

«And the merciful men sailed swiftly by the ancient mound TJERNAGEL»

Tøgdrápa st. 4

Tears of impotent rage by Eirik Storesund

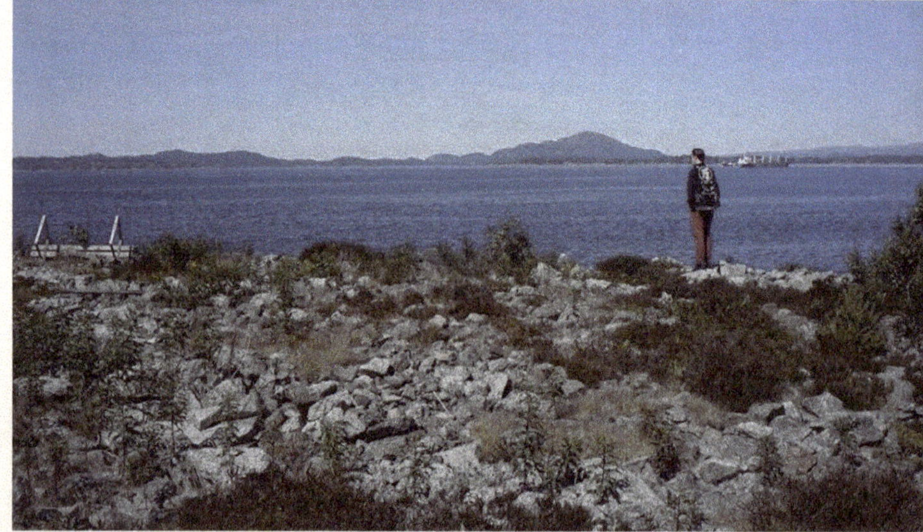

You don't need to go to Bamiyan or Palmyra to see crimes against world heritage: A casual drive through the Norwegian countryside may be enough to convince you how dire things are, and how no ancient sites and monuments can be taken for granted. There we find justification for the Scandifuturist aphorism: To the future there must be a past.

On **Avaldsnes** in Rogaland, a Merovingian Period menhir at Kongshaugen was broken into pieces and turned turned into filler just a few decades ago. At **Tysnes** I have personally seen standing stones that were turned into barn bridges, or toppled for the most banal, yet evergreen reason of human boredom. The **Egge** runestone from Hadeland was subjected to a torrent of harassments between 1866 and 1875, «for the fun of it» as one report claims, before it was ultimately broken into so many pieces it could no longer stand even with iron reinforcements. When the lighthouse at **Ryvarden** was built, it is likely that they took stones from the more ancient nearby beacon, named in the murky past after Flóki Vilgerðarson, the man credited with discovering Iceland. In 1910, a teacher by the name of Dalen notified Bergen Museum about the wanton destruction of the then unregistered hillfort at **Innbjoa**, where local youths amused themselves by rolling the rocks that made up the rampart off the edge of the cliffs.

The same story is retold almost wherever you go in the land of Norway, and this is no coincidence: Something happened somewhere around 1850, or soon before. President of Parliament Wilhelm Christie (1778-1849) noted in his time that many peasants maintained taboos against excavating burial mounds. We can deduce that some break happened. Technology itself does not explain it. At some point there was a cultural and philosophical shift that made sites like these a free-for-all for vandalism. Not only did people destroy these once respected sites at an unprecedented rate: they sometimes did it for sport, to simply pass the time. I believe it was the industrialization, what Inge Krokann so excellently coined **The Great Shapeshift of Norwegian Peasant Society**. That was the process that caused it. Starting with the reform of land subdivision laws in 1827, or even earlier, with the Age of Enlightenment, the process was encouraged by abandonment of Natural Economy, and finally solidified by the mechanization of agriculture. None of these are individually at fault, but come together in a cocktail that paved way for common contemporary disregard for these sites within the Norwegian situation. The result was an unprecedented period of disrespect and destruction of ancient heritage, «simply because», but not without counter-reaction. I can think of no sound reason to explain it sufficiently. Never before had it been easier to cut new slabs for bridges, or live comfortably on the land they had. If there was antipathy against ancient sites, why not 4- or 600 years prior? Never had the destruction of ancient agricultural obstacles seemed less necessary, if that was the point, and yet it was only in the latter half of the 19th century that people began to pull down such ancient mounuments, even Medieval churches, on a noteworthy scale. Seemingly for the abominable sin of rusticity. This would continue until new laws came into place in the latter half of the 20th century, and even then!

My grandfather was a pioneering maritime conservationist in North Rogaland. An organizer and patron of our local culture. And yet when I asked him in the dizzy, final years of his life, if he recalled any specifics about named, lost monuments or burial mounds in our home area it was clear he saw little value in these sites. He was no particular enemy of the past, quite the contrary. In many respects he was a trailblazer of local heritage. And yet, a typical man of his generation, uncaring for, and even bothered by the shackles of the deep past. As a young lorry driver, whether he knew it or not, it is likely that he drove rocks, infamously quarried from age old burial mounds when they extended the road at Avaldsnes for the 700th anniversary of St. Olaf's Church in 1950. Such were the times. If only that was the end of it.

Recall all those unknowable things that are lost as a result of our negligence.

Kari Heie

aka. «Vis-Kari» (b. 1828)

Born:
Flå, Hallingdal

Deeds:
Preacher, mystic, culture driver

One fateful day, the mystic **«Wise-Kari»** collapsed on the church floor. Upon her awakening, she was able to point out in the congregation, each of those who would go to whichever corner of Hell. Fiddles were burned en masse in Numedal after this. Such was usually the case wherever pietists set root and voiced their grievances regarding the atavistic and perceivably pagan ways of the venacular music and dancing. As an ironic consequence in terms of folk music conservation, the area retains a rich recorder tradition, as the flute was not sinful.

- By word of mouth via Kenneth Lien

Runestone Sö 305 «Sibbi and Tjarvi had the stone raised in memory of Torkel, their father.»

Photo by Hilding Mickelsson / Hälsinglands Museum

Art & Poetry

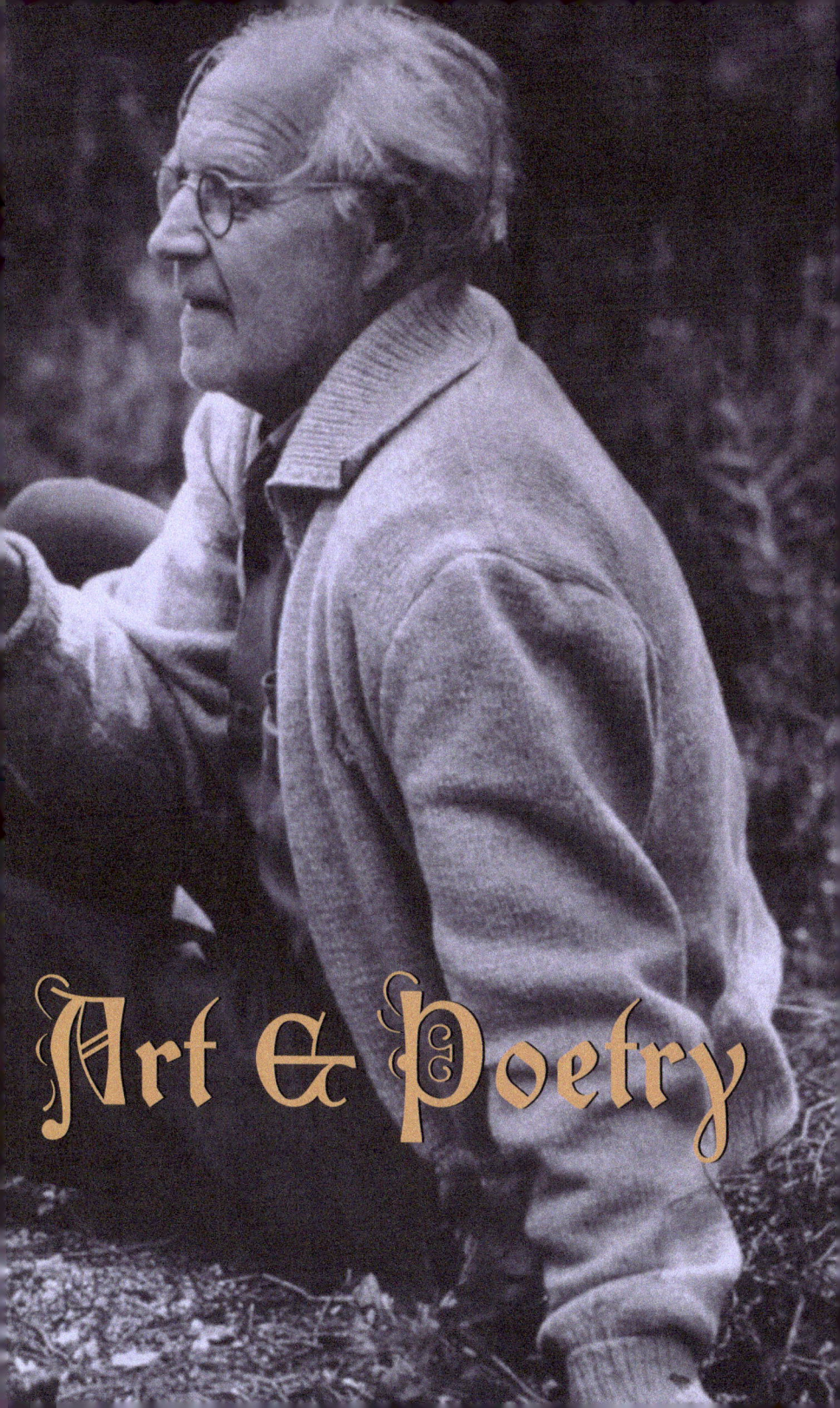

Peter Horneland
peterhorneland.com

ᚼᛆᛂᚿᚠᛁᚿᛏᛆᚴᛆ :ᚢ
HAENFINTAKA :ᚢ
[Ha en fin dag, a :)]

2022
Blithing pole installation
33x114 cm

«Hey Oslo! This is a blithing pole. I turn this blithing pole towards you because I hope that you're having a nice day! And I hope all the folks living here are having a nice day! And I hope all the gnomes, the land-wights, and other spirits who dwell here have a particularly nice day, so that they can help the rest of us to have a nice day! Thank you. Regards, Peter.»

Freely based on Egill Skallgrímsson, Egils saga

Interpret the Runes!

Fartein Th. Øverland has concocted this runic riddle for our enjoyment. Decipher the codeword and send it to us. The first person to uncover its secrets will be prized the original illustration.

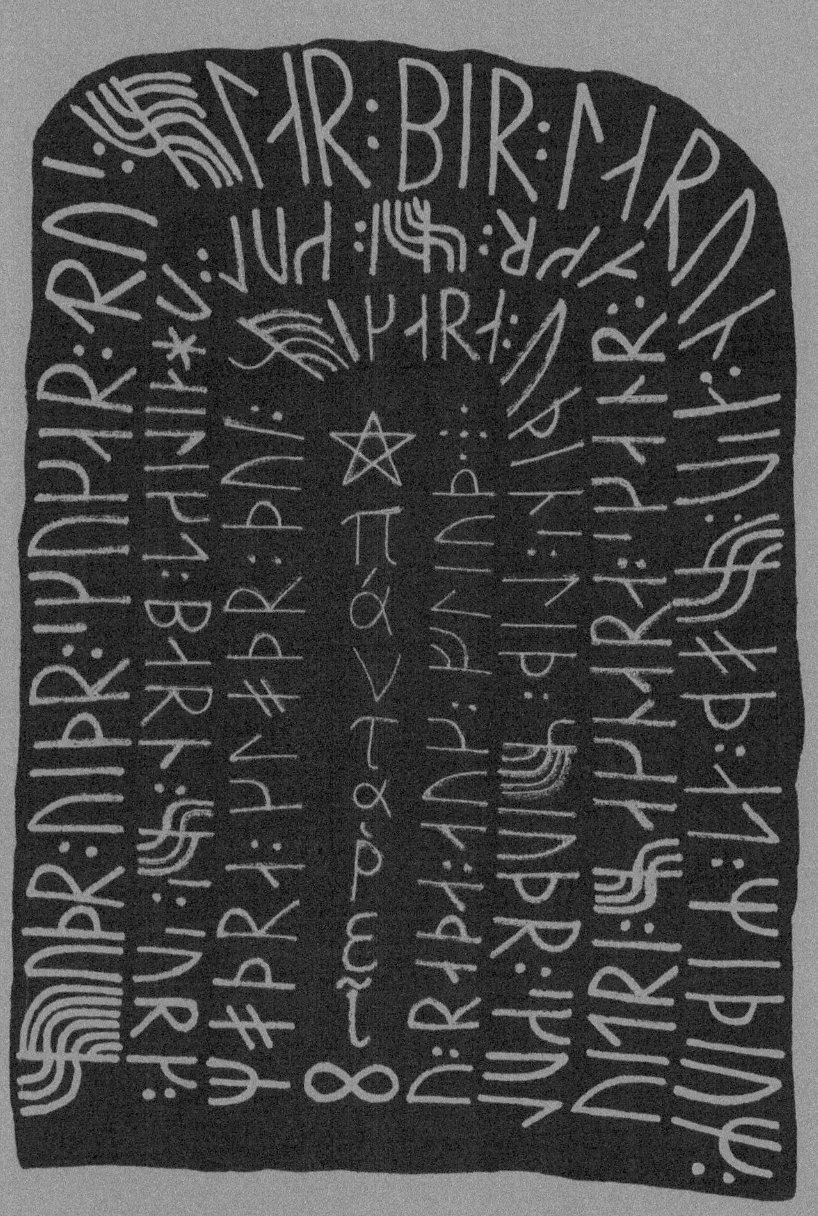

ᚱᛅᚦ:ᚱᚢᚾᛅᛉ:ᚦᛅᛉ:ᚱᛅᚴᛁᚾᚢᚴᚢᛏᚢ

Moondog

Thor and the Midgard Serpent

Thor is the only god who hurls the mighty hammer;
when he hurls it,
thunder and lightning attend.
Calling it Mjölnir,
he hurls it high into the sky.
It hits the worm -the midgardsormr- on the head.
The serpent's sea is foaming red with blood.
Earthquake-maker-monster,
beware each time you take the air!
Though the sea may be your home,
don't break the surface.
You should know by now,
he will hit you again!

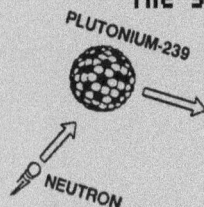

Wrap Ymir's body,
constrict the earth
for all you're worth,
with tail in mouth.
Apply the pressure,
hear it crack.
Volcanoes come
-as geysers come-
from you!

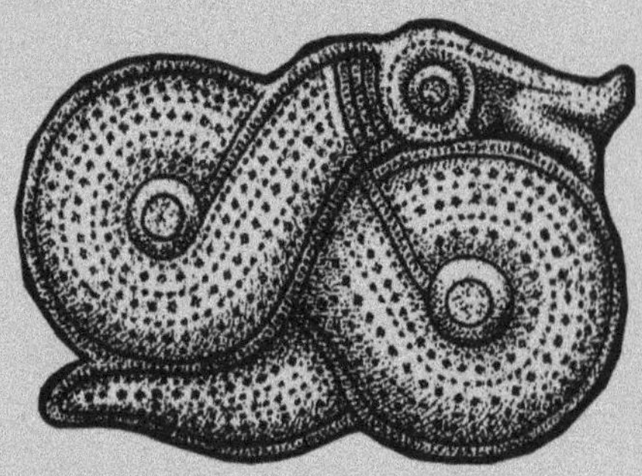

Though you suffer many assaults,
it seems you can't be killed-
either Mjölnir wasn't made for Midgard-serpents,
or your head is harder than heads have to be.
Neither is winning,
for it's a draw!
And there's the flaw:
For man's estate must bear the burden,
come what may.
And more will come,
much more will come its way.
You and Thor will wage total war,
your day is fading fast,
as you fight into the night.

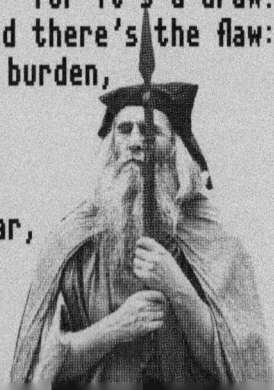

DIMENSION IMPLODER

CHAOS FROM ORDER

D:\SKADINAUJŌ\ II:

BACK TO Nature

STILL
WATER
MAGNUS-ANDRESEN

"HERE, DEEP IN THE FOREST SURROUNDING OSLO, WAITING FOR WEAPONS TO DROP FROM THE SKY, THE WAR SEEMS LIKE A FAR OFF DREAM."

"ONLY THE THOUGHT OF YOU, MY LOVE, KEEPS ME FROM SLIPPING FURTHER AWAY FROM THE WORLD."

"WHEN WILL THIS WAR END? WHEN WILL I SEE YOU AGAIN?"

GERMAN SOLDIERS!

CRACK
RATAT

UH..PLEASE, YOU HAVE TO HELP ME! I NEED TO HIDE FROM THE GERMANS.

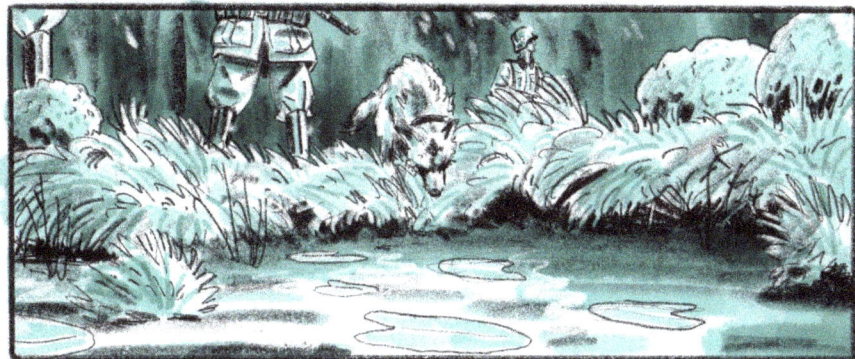

YOU ARE SAFE NOW MY LOVE.

MY LOVE..?

MY LOVE!
BLAGH..

I CURSE YOU! FLEE NOW AND YOU WILL NEVER FIND YOUR LOVE AGAIN! YOU WILL BE LOST FOR ALL TIME!

HAHAHAHAH

A Norwegian seter
(summer mountain pasture)

Spot the cup-marks

Lifestyle

«DIG» YOUR OWN **GRAVE**N MEATS

Not just gravlax! A Nordic delicacy demystified!

Even the devil's great-grandma has heard about gravlax, the scrumptious cured salmon product fawned over in delis across the world (both the young and the old). But did you know that the same principles can be applied to the flesh of just about any animal? The possibilities of home curing are limited only by our divinely gifted imaginations, and whichever animals are legally at your disposal (Use your head. Don't simply go out and knife a porpoise).

While there doesn't seem to be an established English equivalent to the term, the prefix «grav-» refers to «graving», referring literally to the archaic process of burying fish and meat to preserve it (cognate with English «grave»). A curing rub consisting of sugar, salt, and seasoning in combination with cool temperatures and gravity are what makes these «graven» products, which make for a perfect weekend treat that you can easily prepare at home a few days in advance using a simple formula. The seasonings are entirely optional, so feel free to screw around and experiment. A smidgeon of curing salt (Prague powder #2) doesn't hurt. Be mindful not to poison yourself. Game such as (rein)deer, moose or grouse are typical, but lamb, goat, beef and horse do well. But use only lean, choice cuts!

Essential gear:

- 1 platter
- Some kind of weight (platter, chopping board)
- Fridge, cold cellar, fallout shelter, attic etc.

Ingredients per kilo of protein:

100 grams granulated sugar
100 grams salt

1 tablespoon caraway seeds
1 tablespoon dill weed
1 teaspoon cracked juniper berries
1 teaspoon black pepper
1 teaspoon mustard seeds
A shot of aquavit, whiskey, liquor of your choice

Serve sliced alongside your drink of choice, perhaps with a nice mustard sauce?

Directions:

1. Pat your meat clean and dry.
2. Mix all the ingredients of the curing rub in a bowl.
3. Massage the rub evenly into the meat.
4. Transfer the meat over to whatever plate or dish you are using. Adding any remaining rub.
5. Place weight on top of the meat, covering it evenly. You can place a bowl of water or milk carton or other kind of weight on top if you like.
6. Put the whole setup in the fridge and leave it there for two to five days, turning the meat at least once a day to ensure even brining. Some brine the meat in a ziplock bag.

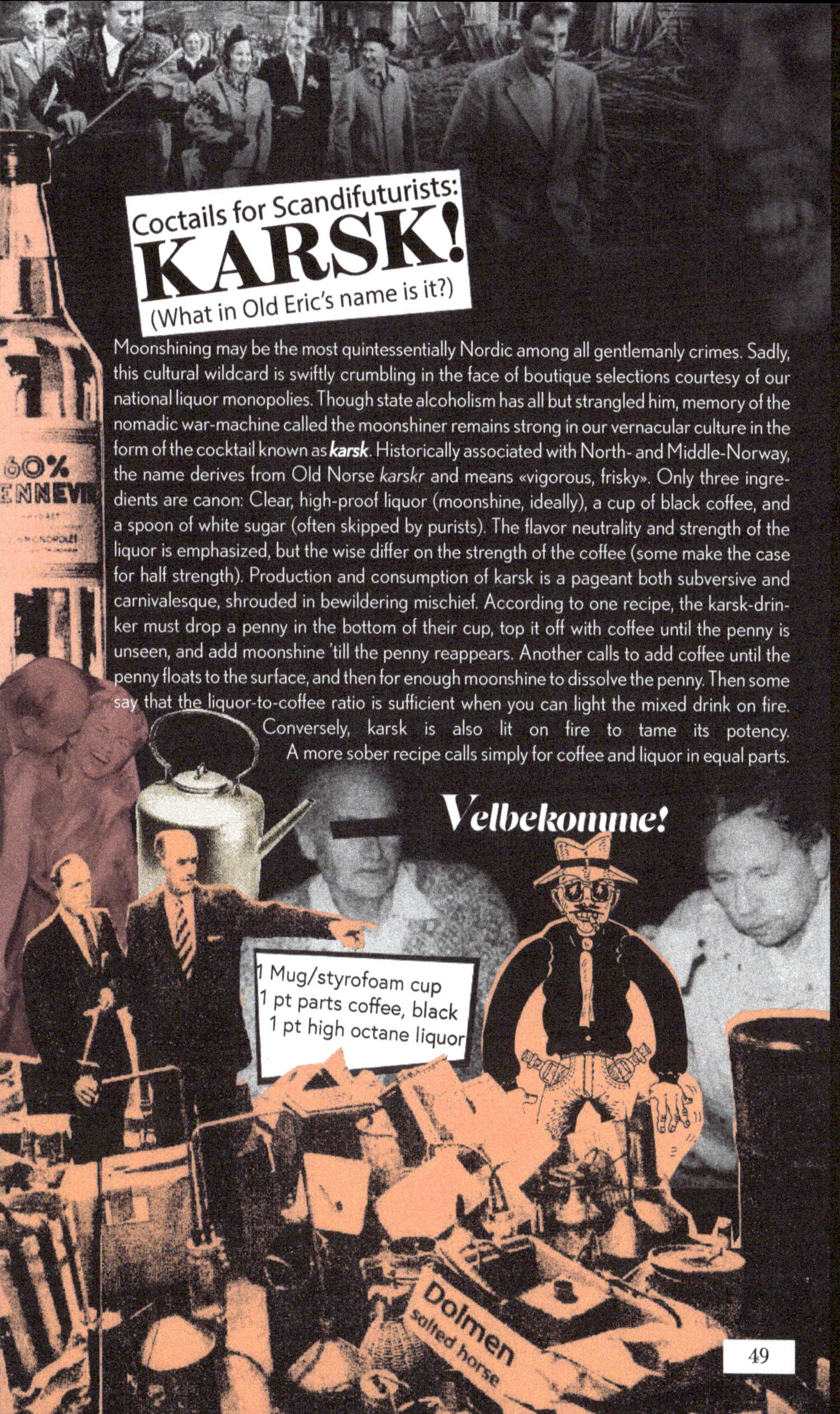

Coctails for Scandifuturists:

KARSK!

(What in Old Eric's name is it?)

Moonshining may be the most quintessentially Nordic among all gentlemanly crimes. Sadly, this cultural wildcard is swiftly crumbling in the face of boutique selections courtesy of our national liquor monopolies. Though state alcoholism has all but strangled him, memory of the nomadic war-machine called the moonshiner remains strong in our vernacular culture in the form of the cocktail known as ***karsk***. Historically associated with North- and Middle-Norway, the name derives from Old Norse *karskr* and means «vigorous, frisky». Only three ingredients are canon: Clear, high-proof liquor (moonshine, ideally), a cup of black coffee, and a spoon of white sugar (often skipped by purists). The flavor neutrality and strength of the liquor is emphasized, but the wise differ on the strength of the coffee (some make the case for half strength). Production and consumption of karsk is a pageant both subversive and carnivalesque, shrouded in bewildering mischief. According to one recipe, the karsk-drinker must drop a penny in the bottom of their cup, top it off with coffee until the penny is unseen, and add moonshine 'till the penny reappears. Another calls to add coffee until the penny floats to the surface, and then for enough moonshine to dissolve the penny. Then some say that the liquor-to-coffee ratio is sufficient when you can light the mixed drink on fire. Conversely, karsk is also lit on fire to tame its potency. A more sober recipe calls simply for coffee and liquor in equal parts.

Velbekomme!

1 Mug/styrofoam cup
1 pt parts coffee, black
1 pt high octane liquor

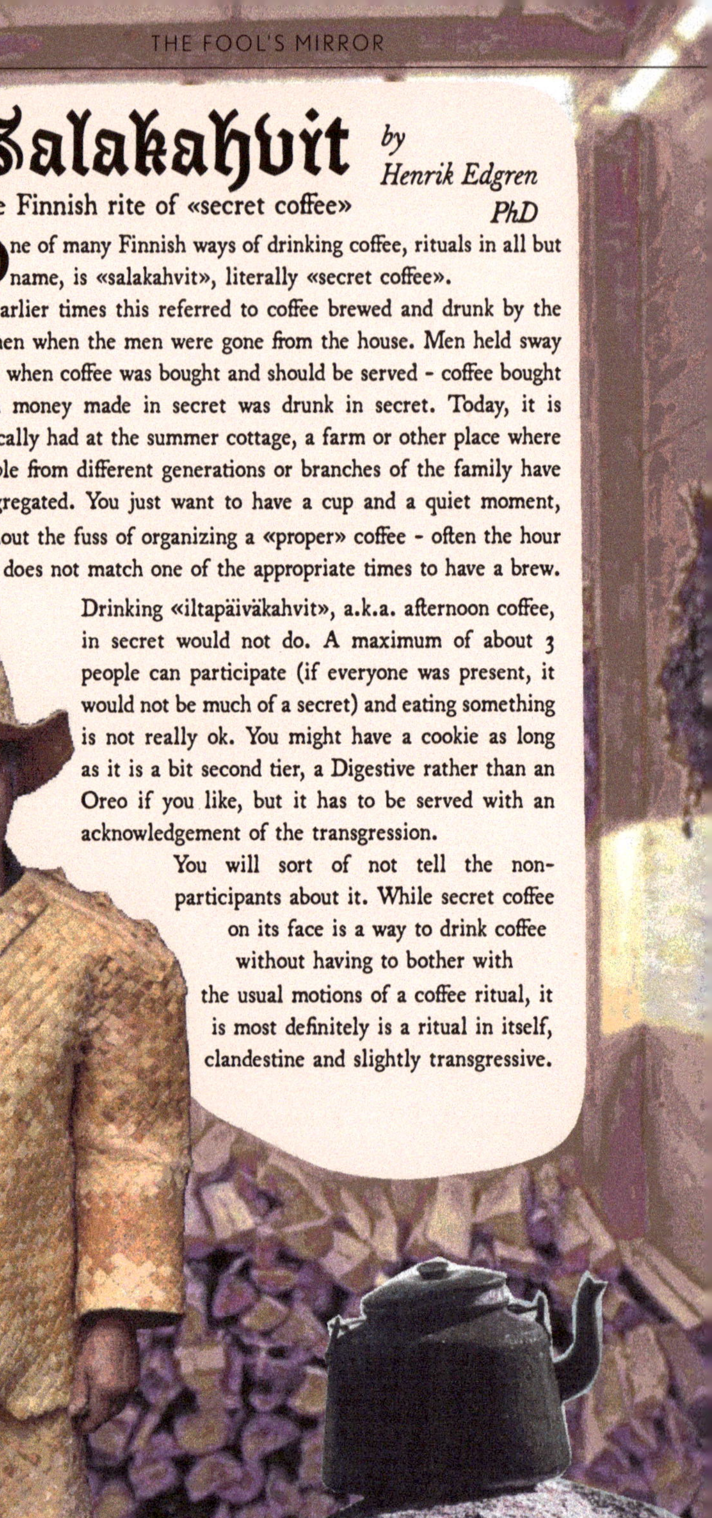

Salakahvit

by Henrik Edgren PhD

The Finnish rite of «secret coffee»

One of many Finnish ways of drinking coffee, rituals in all but name, is «salakahvit», literally «secret coffee». In earlier times this referred to coffee brewed and drunk by the women when the men were gone from the house. Men held sway over when coffee was bought and should be served - coffee bought with money made in secret was drunk in secret. Today, it is typically had at the summer cottage, a farm or other place where people from different generations or branches of the family have congregated. You just want to have a cup and a quiet moment, without the fuss of organizing a «proper» coffee - often the hour also does not match one of the appropriate times to have a brew.

Drinking «iltapäiväkahvit», a.k.a. afternoon coffee, in secret would not do. A maximum of about 3 people can participate (if everyone was present, it would not be much of a secret) and eating something is not really ok. You might have a cookie as long as it is a bit second tier, a Digestive rather than an Oreo if you like, but it has to be served with an acknowledgement of the transgression.

You will sort of not tell the non-participants about it. While secret coffee on its face is a way to drink coffee without having to bother with the usual motions of a coffee ritual, it is most definitely is a ritual in itself, clandestine and slightly transgressive.

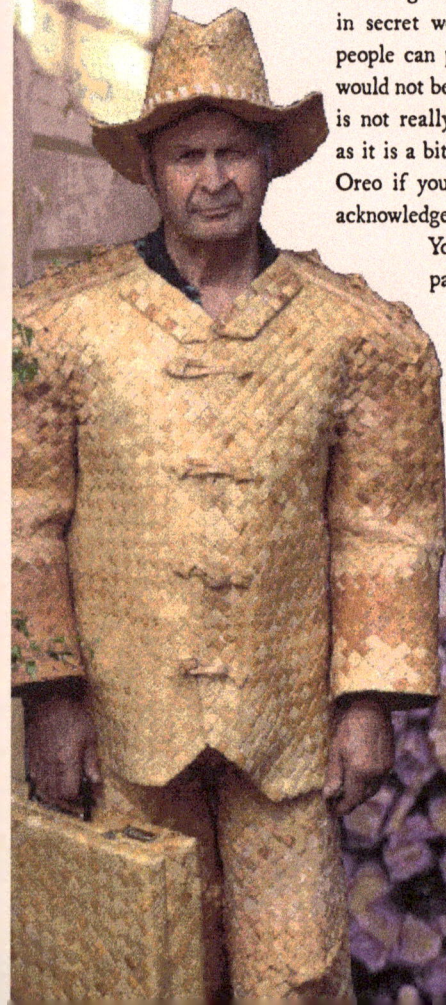

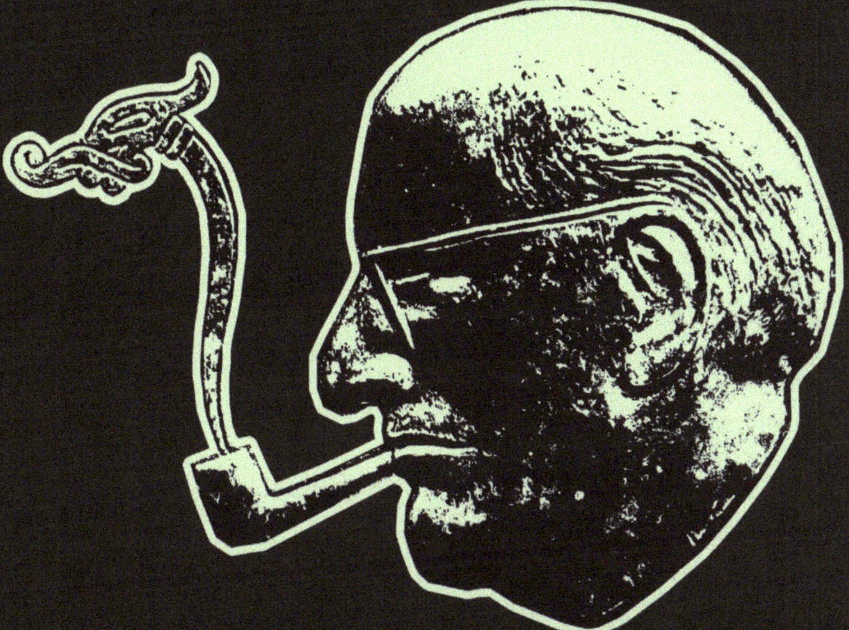

POUR ONE OUT

IF YOU ARE
THIRSTY
SO ARE THEY

This message brought to you by The Council for the Preservation of Little Folks

TAKE A PILGRIMAGE TO

THE ELF-BELLS OF RINGING ROCKS, PA

About an hour and a half north of Philadelphia and the old colony of New Sweden, along the Delaware river, lies Ringing Rocks County Park. Visually it is not much to write home about, unless rocks are your thing. On the surface level, it simply looks like any old boulder field. But don't be fooled! This is a site filled to the brim with subterranean wonder and mystery. You see, as the name implies, the field is full of sonorous rocks which will give off a metallic, bell-like tone if you whack em with a rock or a hammer.

Hence it is no shock that people flock as if by some chthonic compulsion to beat upon these lithophonic boulders with whatever they have on hand, producing petroglyphs that seem like elf-querns in all but name as a side-effect of their primitive, sonorous bashing. Hiking options are ample in the area, but the boulder field itself is merely a five minute stroll from the parking lot by Ringing Rocks Road. Just drive to Upper Black Eddy and you are practically there (curious that there seems to be no Lower Black Eddy. Perhaps that's where the Hidden Folk live). It has often been demonstrated that some that the so-called cup mark petroglyphs and elf-querns of Scandinavia occur on such lithophonic rocks. But it is hard to tell the extent without potentially breaking the law, so this is a rare opportunity to have at it. All within reason, of course!

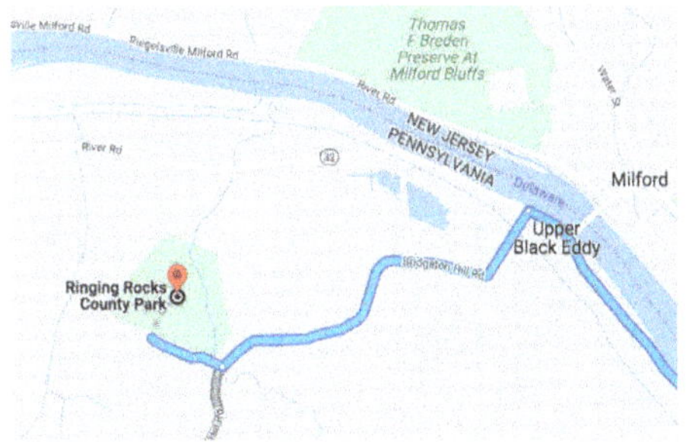

Advice column

TROLLS under YOUR house?

Diógenés Jónsson, PhD

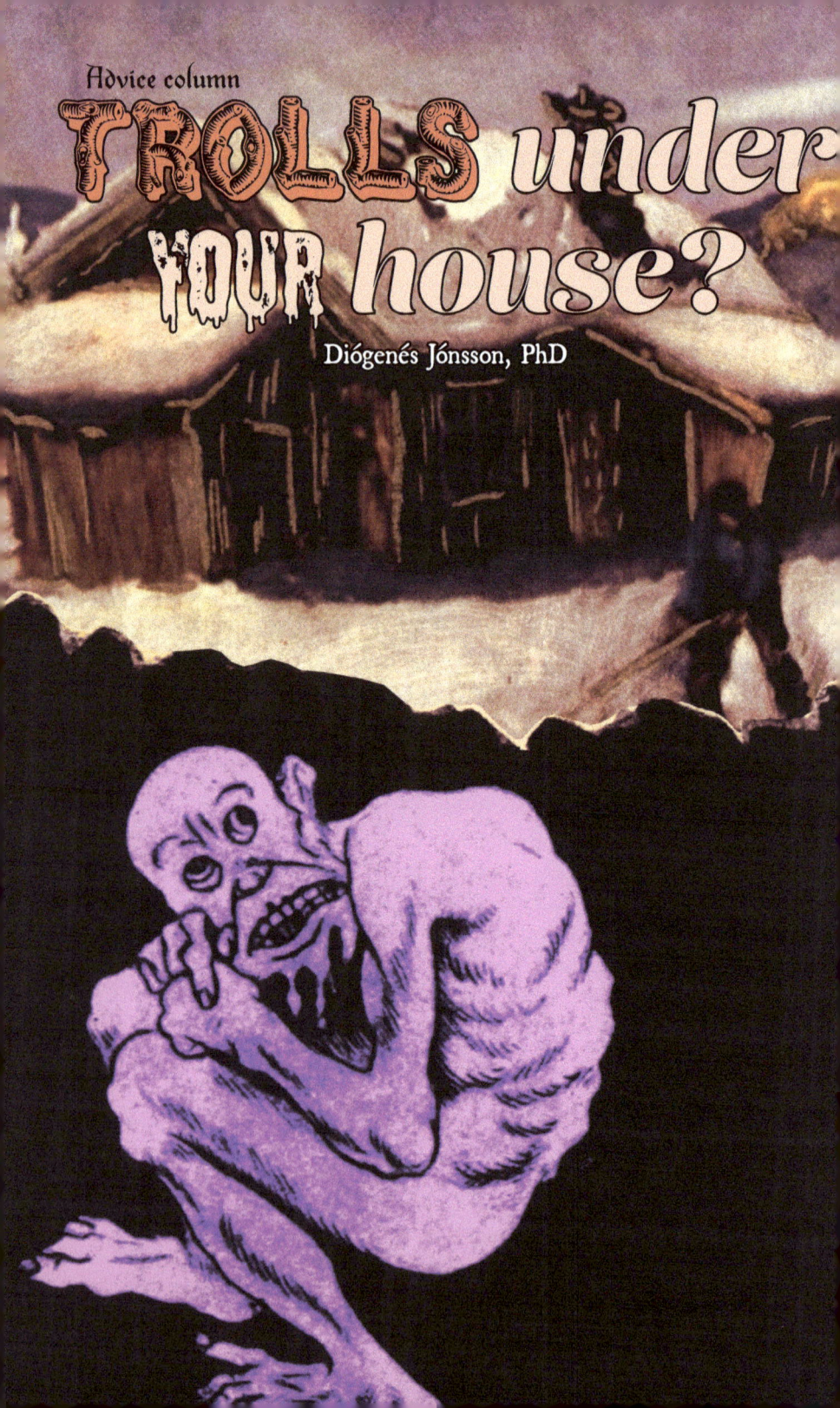

Dear herr Diógenés, PhD, as of late my life has been a living nightmare. I have suffered the most horrendous seizures, my cows milk sour, my wife rode away on a bear, and our first-born was swapped for a horrible goblin that won't stop screaming. I am not usually superstitious, but my neighbor suggests I might have a troll problem on my hands. I smoked out the cowshed, put steel in the crib, painted tar crosses on the porch, but nothing seems to help! How do I remedy this? Is there a specific deity I should appeal to? I want nothing to do with trolls!

Sincerely, Karolius Mogensen

Dumb it may sound, but it could **always** be true: You just might have a serious troll infestation on your feeble, mortal hands. Then again if you don't agree with the premise, that's perfectly natural. Our society is so bankrupt, so stingy in its imagination, and so scared of them, that trolls are denied even the right to exist! To this, as with many such delusions of modern civilization, the **Trollish** remains a defiant middle finger to whatever we think about them. Waste no time on coddled, disenchanted naysayers who traded the divine sparkle of childlike retardation for so-called enlightenment. Their souls and appetite for the fantastic are like bonzai trees in the pot of logical positivism: stunted, mangled, severed from earhtliness. Sad, really. Even in the polar night the day is too damn long to suffer the endwarfment of such hard materialism, but I digress. The one delusion I should first address is one particular golden calf held sacred by any drab cultist of light and clarity: that the lot of man is to strive for divinity. What a comedy. Shake that off immediately, and most of your neuroses will piss off. Your troll problem will never go away, so here is my advice upfront: If you can't beat 'em, join 'em!

Those who know their Eddas would well realize that humanity is divine by design! We parrot the gods all day long, and continue where we left off even in our sleep. The average Ola and Kari aspire for nothing that isn't already divinely ordained, no matter how ambitious or passive that may be. Have you ever heard of someone who dreams all day long of laying face up in the mires? To be the mire? Or to be slowly eroded by the wind and rain across the span of a thousand winters? Show me *one* well-adjusted person with aspirations of living beneath a rock while he thirsts for the blood of the baptized. Most people are content with television binges and Chinese take-out. As the gods intended! Let's take a look at some of the «achievements» the gods have inspired, shall we? Take dogs, for example. The evolutionary equivalent to a high school bully slamming a dweeb into the locker of cultivation across the span of thousands of years. Cruel, it is!

The foundations on which these impulses rest are of the same nature that compels humanity to look to the stars. The couch potato and the body builder are the same animal, and only the vanity of small difference says otherwise. If I must speak the silent part out loud, there is little else to this primordial cargo cult called culture, but the tragic shared fate of human-divine co-morbidity. Dead ringers are we to the gods in all their ingenious, clumsy, self-serving, two-faced, cousin-fucking ways. Striving for their likeness is redundant, and that is our gallow to hang on, friends! If this isn't the reality check you were hoping for, why don't you do us all a favor and vanish in the mountain. If you are ready to face the trolls, read on.

I worship the glass half-full! Adore it! The gods left us to fester in this ontological compost bin and walled themselves off from the mess they created, blushing, realizing all too well the shortcomings of themselves and their work, but that is no reason to be a lousy neighbor to our Trollish half-kin. Have you perhaps considered what you might have done to provoke these subterranean reactions? Maybe *you* are the bully? None of this would have happened, had you never been born. Take this history lesson: the gods weren't satisfied with the pre-cosmic order, and turned their frowns upside down by upending Ginnungagap's primordial circus. But trollhood remembers the genocidal conquest of the gods, and the gods are reminded of this recollection every time they have been forced to deal with the occasional titanic interloper looking to bed a goddess. By neccessity the gods became pragmatic. More often than not, the gods struck short-sighted bargains with the used car salesmen of the ogreish ne'er-do-wells and Thursian mobsters. Inevitably, sooner or later, before you know it, this will bite them in their divine asses. They made the bed and shat in it, to loosely paraphrase the *Völuspá*. *Grímr*, the vagrant god eponymous to the poem *Grímnismál*, prophesized in his own sexy lill' way that the the skies will split apart, and fire consume the mountains and the sea. For this chain of events there is none to blame but those who got us into this mess in the first place. The sons of blazing Muspell will ride and claim their due from the children of *Búri*, with interest! Tragic it may be. Comically so. They get no sympathy here.

Anyway, we, the sons and daughters of ❤Ash + Elm❤ have enough on our hands trying to avoid regressing into utter trolldom. I can smell the piss-stench of your resistance even through your email. You fear your own shadow. Remember that in spite of all their intolerance of trollkind, the gods were not above X-ing and Y-ing their subterranean brains out, yielding many an XX, and many an XY (give or take an X or Y or two). This, combined with the fact that both gods and trolls have been buggering mankind since the days where we slept in the trees, I think the implications go without saying. It's in our blood, waiting for the right time and conditions to germinate. To do what comes natural. To disregard, even subvert polite society!

There are many things I would rather do instead of writing this dumb response to you, for example. None of which are conducive to great and honorable deeds, or even wise to mention on the record, let alone in daylight. For sure, the weaker my spark of divine flame, the greater the pull of sleeping under bridges and haunt the subways like a wailing ghost. But oppositely, I think it is better that way, than to lean into the denial of NATURE that the divine and anthropocentric world seeks to cultivate and engender, especially those who take the gods but all too seriously. Truth be spoken, I feel a duty to act in solidarity with those who have succumbed to this trollish impulse. Our most ancient, but also least flattering heritage. One that taints even the pantheon, let's recall! After the gods, the greatest heroes and poets of ancient Scandinavia had trollish folk in their immediate ancestry. Cross-pollination between the poles of this tension-pair are necessary. The mutant as the ultimate creative principle. A principle older than the hills, back to the age before ages, to Ymir and his kin. So let that be clear, Sir and/or Madam, that this is no dichotomy of the Abrahamic sort. If you are looking for those sunbeams of shame to cast upon our bridge-Troll brethren, you will get none from me.

So, what would I do in your situation. Perhaps you can atone by the cult of the Trollish? To be fair, let's not kid ourselves and think that these primordial ogres were worshipped side by side with

«The Scandifuturist ~~must~~ should recognize at least the possibility that there are landscapes besides, beyond, under, over, and in-between whichever place the the crow flies, or the cat drags into.»

the gods in opulent temples. Our ancestors may not have **worshipped** ogres, wights, and trolls. But did they commune with them? Appease them? ...Kiss them? Lie with them as a man does with a woman? Or indeed as some lie with each other, in various configurations? Our ancestors freely admitted it themselves, that such things were not out of the realm of possibility. Nor were they adverse to give them offerings of food, coins, of grease and trinkets. Who can blame them for getting lonely while the gods were away on business? Gods may come and go, but the Trollish remains a worldly constant. The Trollish is the awkward hometown, the mole on your face, or a dark secret in the family. The Thursian mafia in the Godly police state. You'd better make peace with it, the sooner the better.

Gods have whims and passing fascinations, one day hot, one day cold. They never could decide what they wanted to achieve, and we inherited their dissatisfaction. On lukewarm trolls you can depend. Moreover: We're the ones who have to deal with these these subterranean neighbors, whatever name they go by, whichever shape they take. I'm of the opinion that it is better to be a good neighbor than a bad one, and so we must pay offerings to these agents of the genius loci. And lip service to their natural thuggery.

Icelandic Hidden Folk are often treated to luxury condos

Man is a curious beast, but despite our desire to know, the exact taxonomy of the chthonic denizen is the least relevant part of dealing with it. Troll in a strict sense of «grotesque inhumanoid» or a less specific, more flattering one, as we see when it refers to the Hidden Folk, and various, more or less spectral entities, or things that evade direct classification more generally. «The Weird». These categories are arbritrary, more a spectrum really. You don't know what you're dealing with half the time, and it's not as if you can take their word at face value either. It's better not to ask.

The Scandifuturist must recognize at least the possibility that there are landscapes besides, beyond, under, over, and in-between whichever place the the crow flies, or the cat drags into. That startlingly often, their omnipresent liminal spaces are bottlenecks of critters both pesky and obscene. It's at the threshold of such vistas that the rite of the **Troll Toll** must be exercised. Pennies, liquor, and scraps of food go far to appease - even impress - the subterraneans, so called, who live in the cracks and crevices, nooks and crannies of the countryside, village, city, underpass, gas station, space station, you name it. Uff da, no space is too sacred, or too profane. They congregate in sinkholes and garbage chutes, trash cans, cracked walls and hidden compartments. Under rugs and between the floors, in crossroads and subway tracks, and beneath auspicious rocks. In secret gardens, attics, fountains, caverns, graves, underground streams, sewers, folleys, drains, ditches and derelict houses. In phone booths and bridges, manholes, potholes and assholes. Leave in these places spare change, joss paper, hell money and minis of liquor. Or pour before them libations and accoutrements of friendly words and adoration, and they - whether Hulder Nation or Thursian Mafia, be they called the Hidden People, the Garbage Elves, the Mole Folk,

Fair Folk, may they be appeased!
Even kitchen scraps, offal, bacon grease, cooking oil, yeast slurry, and bottle dregs are suitable offerings. A hot dog, strategically placed, will get you far. The wise often contend that intent is what truly makes offerings offerings and sacrifices sacrifices. Normally, if it is within your means to sacrifice one adequate thing, it is a shame to offer up a cheaper alternative. And if you do not have the means for the nobler sacrifice, the lesser alternative will suffice. This is by all means true when dealing with those pesky and picky eaters called gods, and not necessarily irrelevant when dealing with trolls and the Hidden Folk either. But in the end it is all about giving something that is suitable, «in the spirit of the sacrifice» so to speak. The bar of suitability for Troll Tolls and offerings to spirits of place is, thankfully, abysmal. These are opportunistic entities that will often accept, even take whatever comes their way. I would never bring a piece of burnt toast to the temple, but the sordid creature that lives beneath my stairs is probably what caused my distraction that caused the burning of the toast to begin with, and so it is conceivable that the smoke spilling out of my kitchen was its way of demanding gratification of its subterannean senses. If we don't give, they often just come and take it anyway, eating our bread crumbs and licking our spoons while we sleep, or trip us in order to make us spill our drinks. Don't even get me started on the depraved appetites of the wretched piss elves, known by their ominous rattling in the cistern or pipes behind the urinals. But if you proactively seek to give even the most measly of offerings, NEVER catch them off guard. Don't simply pour cooking oil over their abodes without warning or expression of intent, if you value your life. Many a man would have been spared a red and swollen tallywhacker if they had only cried «here's you due!» before relieving themselves.

You should discern the lay of the land: Don't expact some grand return. What you are really doing is maintaining a relationship. A relative absence of misery and illness should be reward enough. And if you're miserable and ill already, I figure you have nothing to lose. Consider it at best a subscription service for possible chthonic goodwill, or a ritual for the conjuration of novelty. Sometimes it is even a matter of giving so that they *do not give*! Do ut non des! Protection money is what it really is, staving off the ire of our extra-dimensionally priviledged frenemies. To be completely candid, I'd rather have for neighbor one of those uncanny folk of trollish adjacency than some straight up ogre grotesque. Either of which are easily repelled (or angered) with a church bell, but this I do not advise. Instead, lean into the Wyrd! Bring peculiarly shaped rocks into your yard and hail them as your secret deities! Smear them with butter and cod liver oil, and always leave behind some berries and whatever else you forage behind, as tribute to their king, in some charismatic place!

Good luck, asshole!

Do you have questions for Diógenés Jónsson, PhD?

Write him a letter at Diogenesjonsson@protonmail.com
He just might bother answering.

The doctor reserves the right to embellish and twist the words of any and all submissions.

Weddings & Funerals

Village gossip from all over Scandinavia

HEDMARK: A little bird sung to us that Audun Grautmosæther, a fresh recruit at Rena army base was recently dragged into the mountain by a lovesick hulder-woman. The airforce sweeped the hillsides with helicopters (church bells in tow), but the boy could not be saved. A subterranean chant was intercepted, apparently a statement from the Hidden Nation: «If you can't handle us at our worst, you don't deserve us at our best.» We wish the lovebirds a happy marriage, but won't count on it!

GAUSDAL: Renowned blacksmith and infamous local bachelor, Gjermund on-the-marshes died! Seems the devil finally had the last laugh. The rest of us might have to cross over to the next valley to get our horses shod, unless there are Travelers about. The Fools Mirror sent our editorial staff to pay our respects. The fiddler played like the Old Eric himself was on his tail (he probably was) and the ale was not bad either. Shame the man can't die twice! Bring a date!

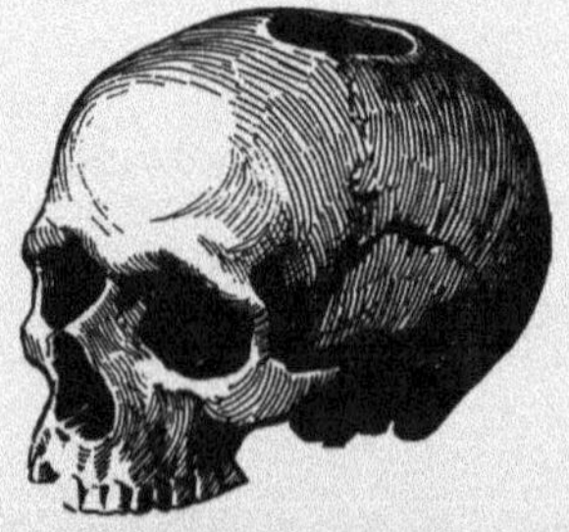

The Boy Who Had Such a Terrible Thing

An erotic fairy tale from Norway

Once upon a time there were three greedy brothers who demanded their inheritance upfront, but their pa wouldn't give it to them before his time. They whined and whined and when their father tired of their whining he gave them their inheritance. The eldest two took their money and went trading, but the youngest, Ashfarter, invested his money in pails of butter. Ashfarter lay by the hearth and buttered his tallywhacker, tilling and rearing it until it grew so great and big and fat that it was rather uncouth. He coiled it three times around his waist, and then his brothers came home. «So there you are, you layabout, you!» They said to Ash-Farter. «Look here what money we earned. You could have it just as good if you had only bothered to join us, you pig-beast!»

Well, Ashfarter lay and listened to their yacking for a while, but then he rolled over and set off to the inn. There he sat and drank and played cards with the old tavern maid, and placed a wager of 600 daler that he could satisfy her in bed. He settled in, uncoiled his thing and then they were off. They started out in the bed in the main hall, and so they they kept at it until they tumbled out and onto the floor, through the door, and down the stairs, through the hallway and down a steep hillside a bit further from the houses. So stingy were they that neither wanted to retire, and so they kept going. The ground at the bottom of the hill was wet and boggy, and soon Ashfarter rolled her down into a soggy pit in the mire as he charged on, but the tavern lady refused to surrender. Then Ashfarter called up to the inn: «You'd better go fetch my coat, I expect to have work here for the winter!». But when the missus heard this she got scared, and said: «Oh no, I better cease now. I've lost.» And so the Ash-Farter won his 600 daler.

Before they arrive at your nightstand, all fairy tales have been through an editorial process. Very often this process began as it went through the meat grinder of oral to literary transmission, and you can only imagine where it went from there. Ironically, many vernacular tales were deemed too vulgar for common consumption. And so as to not upset urban burghers, they were censored or rewritten. The above is not even particularly bad as far as erotic fairy tales go. Another, «The Princess that No-one Could Silence», is known and loved by all Norwegian children. There, all who court the eponymous princess are bested by her sarcastic remarks, and thereby fail to woo her. When they say «Isn't it hot in here?», she answers every time with a laconic «It's hotter in the cinders over there.»
What they didn't tell us was the original, unredacted reponse: «It's hotter in my ass.»

Have a *Great* Blót!

How? With **Dolmen®** brand Salted Horse, of Norse!

Make this full moon feast a divinely blessed delight with Dolmen® brand ceremonial grade Salted Horse. Whey cured for old time's sake.

Leave the guts to us!

PRODUCT RECALL

DOLMEN® SALTED HORSE

Customers who have purchased Dolmen® Salted Horse with batch numbers between #20 and #7034 are encouraged to return their items due to the presence of undeclared lutefisk. This is unrelated to the ongoing feud and associated sabotage. The staff at our lutefisk plant has been outlawed and we hope to have the incident rectified by next year. On behalf of the Dolmen® family, please accept our sincerest apoligies.

- The **Dolmen®** public relations office

Where To Dine

SMORGASBORD
The largest Scandinavian Smorgasbord Restaurant in the U. S.
OPEN LUNCH & DINNER 7 DAYS A WEEK
CHILDREN'S MENU
EXCELLENT FACILITIES FOR CATERING IN BEAUTIFUL PRIVATE BANQUET ROOMS
ORGAN—PIANO MUSIC NITELY BY JACKIE GLYNN
Credit Cards
Mr. & Mrs. Erik Larsen, Owners
Go Scandinavian at our Super Delicious Smorgasbord at the Beautiful Royal Viking
Skoal!
ROYAL VIKING
Jericho Turnpike
Woodbury, L.I., N.Y.
(516) WA 1-6510
WA 1-6511

EAT LIKE A NORSE
NEW YORK'S MOST DISTINCTIVE SCANDINAVIAN RESTAURANT
SMÖRGÅSBORD
LUNCHEON • DINNER • SUPPER
EVERY DAY AND SUNDAY TOO!
THE SCANDIA
45th STREET WEST OF BROADWAY
IN THE HOTEL PICCADILLY

Baikingu「古墳」

「Komle-torsdag」!

「Lutefisk musubi」!

スカンジナビアと日本のフュージョン料理。楽しもう!!!

1-8-10 Soto kanda, Chiyoda-ku, Tokyo

MOONSHINE STILLS

Accept no substitutes: do as they do in jolly Trøndelag. We have finally succeeded in manufacturing a better distilliaton apparatus than hitherto thought possible, and we owe it all to our patented *Odic Force®*!

This means a sleeker, more practical design, and optimum results!

Cry not over spilt liquor: Detailed instruction manual included.

.... Liturgical gr. reflux still	600	kr
.... Dam. steel spitoon	200	kr
.... 500 l steel fermenter	1500	kr
.... 50 kg dry turbokveik	150	kr
.... Free product catalog	20	kr

Sum:................

(Postage not Included)

Name:....................................

Address:................................

PO# & Place:.........................

☐ YES I also want an exclusive 300 piece VHS box set of

Reallexikon der Germanischen Altertumskunde

For ONLY 49 kr

YOU SHOULD HAVE LISTENED...

TO BRUTE NORSE

A Scandifuturist podcast about Nordic apocrypha, wyrd Scandinaviana, & ancient eldritchness.
By Old Norse philologist Eirik Storesund

The most stylish clay pots are sold by D. Jonsson & sons

Handmade in Rogaland using only **local** asbestos, unglazed and peat fired at low temperatures for that carbonized look! Give your meals the ancient touch, from D. Jonsson & Sons.
Ondemaen 56, 5522 Åkra

FISCHER

ROLLING TOBACCO

Signature blend with virgin cod liver oil.

Changelings exchanged, no questions asked.
Call: 1-800-Bᛦ11ᛁᚦᚹ

Bósa saga ok Herrauðs : A Norse legendary romance for adults

FOR THE FIRST TIME IN DANISH BY TORMOD TORFAEUS

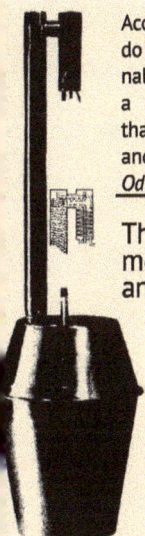

"So one day Odin gets tah thinkin' it'd be a wicked good idea tah commit suicide"

After 800 years, the final installment of *The Edda Trilogy* has at long last arrived!

Picking up where its medieval forebears, *The Poetic Edda* and *The Prose Edda*, left off, *The Impudent Edda* not only introduces readers to a fresh, new perspective on both familiar and previously unknown narratives of Norse mythology, but also brings the world's foremost epic fantasy trilogy to its inevitable and fateful conclusion: in an alleyway behind a dive bar in Boston.

Norse Mythology for Bostonians: A Transcription of the Impudent Edda

Transcribed with an Introduction and Notes by ROWDY GEIRSSON

Highlights of the book include these enthralling episodes of archaic Scandinavian lore and esoteric knowledge:

Old Norse Astrophysics

The Original Gandalf was a Maggot

Odin Commits Suicide

Thor Begets the Green Monster

The Night Freyja Walked the Streets

Odin Experiments with Public Vagrancy

Sad, Flaccid Sex God

Thor Breaks and Enters into a Dunkin' Donuts ...and many more!

CINDERELLA TAVERN DA
OKTOBER-NOVEMBER
BUON APPETITO
Meny
SMALA-
-HOVE-
M/TILBH.
* 199,-
IVAR
VOSS

www.ingramcontent.com/pod-product-compliance
Lightning Source LLC
Chambersburg PA
CBHW050024090426
42734CB00021B/3416

9798986343006